TIME
FOR KIDS®

CONFIDENT 3 READER

Science Scoops

Volcanoes!

By the Editors of TIME FOR KIDS
WITH JEREMY CAPLAN

HarperCollins*Publishers*

About the Author: Jeremy Caplan is a reporter for TIME Magazine. He has written articles for TIME and TIME FOR KIDS® about social issues, nature, and geography. The author is an avid violinist, athlete, and cook. He lives in New York City—far away from any volcano.

To my mother and father, for their love and guidance.

Special thanks to volcanologist Catherine Hickson for sharing her expertise.   —J.C.

Library of Congress Cataloging-in-Publication Data is available.

ISBN-10: 0-06-078223-4 (pbk.) — ISBN-10: 0-06-078224-2 (trade)
ISBN-13: 978-0-06-078223-8 (pbk.) — ISBN-13: 978-0-06-078224-5 (trade)

2 3 4 5 6 7 8 9 10
First Edition

Photography and Illustration Credits:
Cover: Aguilar Patrice—Alamy; cover inset: Getty Images; cover front flap: Jim Sugar—Corbis; title page: Krafft/Photo Researchers; contents page: Tui De Roy—Minden; contents page (top): Carsten Peter—National Geographic; pp. 4–5: Daniel Aguilar—Reuters/Corbis; pp. 6–7: Lon Tweeten; pg. 6 (inset): Scott Taylor—US Navy; pp. 8–9: Karen Kasmauski—National Geographic; pg. 8 (inset): Kennan Ward—Corbis; pp. 10–11: Explorer/Photo Researchers; pp. 12–13: Douglas Peebles—Corbis; pg. 13 (inset): Jim Kauahikaua; pp. 14–15: Zainal Effendie—AP; pg. 14 (inset): courtesy Advanced Ceramic Research; pp. 16–17: Carsten Peter—National Geographic; pp. 18–19: Culliganphoto/Alamy; pg. 18 (inset): Corbis; pp. 20–21: Pictor International/ImageState/Alamy; pg. 21 (inset): Joseph Lertola; pp. 22–23: Gary Braasch—Corbis; pg. 23 (inset): John Berg; pp. 24–25: Alberto Garcia—Corbis; pp. 26–27: Roger Ressmeyer—Corbis; pg. 26 (inset): Roger Harding Picture Library Ltd./Alamy; pp. 28–29: FLPA/Alamy; pg. 29 (inset): Ernst Haas—Getty Images; pp. 30–31: Charles O'Rear—Corbis; pg. 31 (inset): Ralph White—Corbis; pg. 32 (active): Douglas Peebles—Corbis; pg. 32 (dormant): Culliganphoto/Alamy; pg. 32 (extinct): Kennan Ward—Corbis; pg 32 (lava): Explorer/Photo Researchers; pg. 32 (magma): Lon Tweeten; pg. 32 (tectonic plate): Joseph Lertola; pg. 32 (cinder cone): J. Lowenstern—USGS; pg. 32 (stratovolcano): Charles O'Rear—Corbis; pg. 32 (lava dome): Doug Beghtel—The Oregonian/Corbis; pg. 32 (shield volcano): Lyn Topinka—USGS

Acknowledgments:
For TIME FOR KIDS: Editorial Director: Keith Garton; Editor: Nelida Gonzalez Cutler; Art Director: Rachel Smith; Designer: Sarah Micklem; Photography Editor: Jill Tatara

 Check us out at www.timeforkids.com

CONTENTS

Lava spews out of Cerro Azul on the Galapagos Islands.

CHAPTER ONE

The Earth's

KABOOM!

Popocatépetl in
Mexico acts up.

Chimney

Flaming hot rocks spew from the peak. Glowing, red lava bursts out and flows down the mountain. A volcano is erupting!

Take a look at Mount Saint Helens.

A volcano erupts when pressure builds up underground. Hot liquid rock called magma pushes up toward the top of the mountain. As it rises, it creates more and more pressure. When the magma gets to the top, it bursts out as lava.

Mount Saint Helens is in Washington. In 2004 it started to rumble. Scientists fear it will erupt.

BOILING OVER: Steam, other gases, and ash are released at the top of the dome.

CRATER: The opening at the top of the mountain is called the crater.

LAVA DOME: This is a cap of cooled magma that is fixed like a cork in a bottle. When the pressure gets too high, the mountaintop pops.

SHAKING UP: Pressure from magma and hot gases cracks the mountain's rocks. The magma's heat boils groundwater, creating steam.

TIGHT FIT: The magma is squeezed upward like thick toothpaste through a narrow tube. When it gets to the top, it bursts out as lava.

UP AND OUT: As magma rises, it pushes rocks aside. Pressure builds toward an eruption.

MAGMA: The melted rock collects underground. Pressure forces it to the surface.

Mount Kenya in Africa is an extinct volcano.

Volcanoes can be active, dormant, or extinct.

There are more than 1,500 active volcanoes. They can erupt at any time. Dormant volcanoes have not erupted for many years. But these sleeping giants can still explode. Extinct volcanoes have not erupted for thousands of years. They are no longer a threat.

Japan's Mount Fuji is
a dormant volcano.

CHAPTER TWO

Volcano

A scientist in a heat-resistant suit explores Kilauea volcano in Hawaii.

Hunters

Scientists who study volcanoes are called volcanologists. They watch for signs of activity. Volcanologists measure a mountain's every shudder. They look for rock movement, gas, or a rise in temperature at the top of the volcano. These are clues that an explosion may happen.

Researchers take a close look at an eruption in Hawaii Volcanoes National Park.

Studying volcanoes is dangerous work.

Eruptions can come as a big surprise. After years at rest, volcanoes sometimes explode with sudden violence.

Meet a Volcanologist

Jeff Wynn is master of the mountains! He has spent many years studying volcanoes. Wynn is the head of the United States Geological Survey's Volcano Hazards Program. His job is to help the government keep track of volcanic activity. His team of scientists sends out a warning if a volcano looks as if it is getting ready to blow.

Wynn's team travels around the world. "We send scientists to visit volcanoes and learn about them," says Wynn. But studying an active volcano can be dangerous. "We have new ways of watching a volcano without getting too close," he says. "It's exciting, but you have to be careful."

New tools have made it safer to study volcanoes.

These instruments help scientists study the mountains from a distance. Microphones pick up rumbles. Planes gather information. Even satellites in space watch over volcanoes.

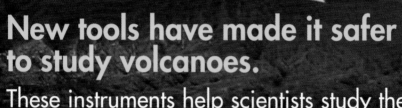

This pilotless plane takes pictures and videos and collects samples of the air.

A volcanologist in Indonesia monitors Mount Bromo.

CHAPTER THREE

The Top Hot Spots

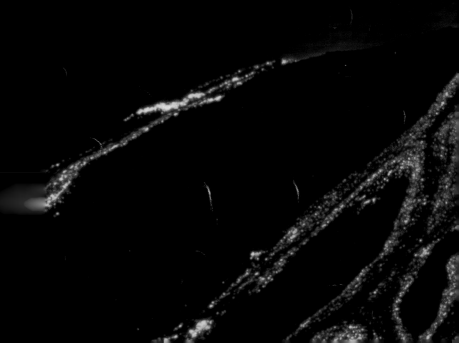

unt Etna in Italy has been called the ndly giant because of its size and beauty. ecent years Etna has been bursting with ivity. At times, streams of hot lava flow vn the mountain. Scientists believe that the ndly giant is becoming more dangerous.

Mount Etna is almost 11,000 feet tall.

BOOM!

Mount Vesuvius looms over Pompeii.

A plaster cast of a victim of the eruption in 79 A.D.

Italy's Mount Vesuvius is a dangerous volcano.

It has erupted more than twenty times. In 79 A.D. it exploded suddenly, burying the nearby city of Pompeii. The lava and volcanic ash preserved the people's homes, writing, and artwork. These ruins are still studied today.

Many volcanoes are in the Ring of Fire.

This belt around the Pacific Ocean outlines a tectonic plate, a piece of the earth's crust. Volcanoes are partly caused by the shifting of plates. Earthquakes are also frequent in the ring.

Surtsey

EUROPE

Mount Vesuvius

Mount Etna

AFRICA

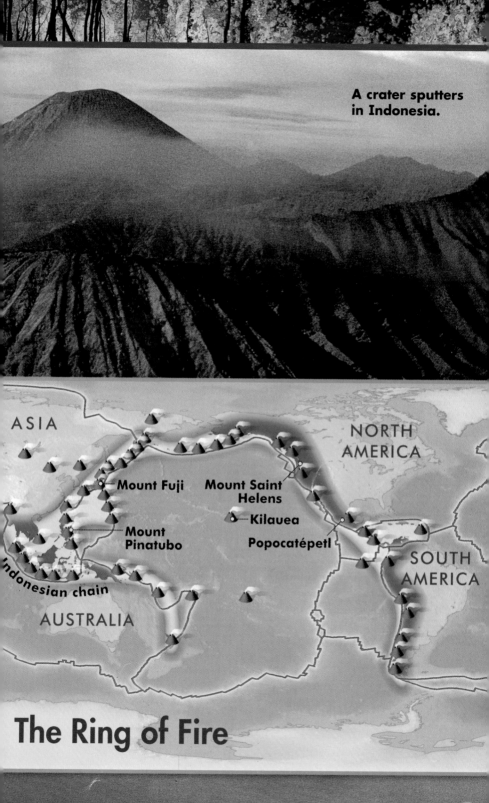

A crater sputters
in Indonesia.

ASIA

NORTH
AMERICA

Mount Fuji

Mount Saint
Helens

Mount
Pinatubo

Kilauea

Popocatépetl

Indonesian chain

SOUTH
AMERICA

AUSTRALIA

The Ring of Fire

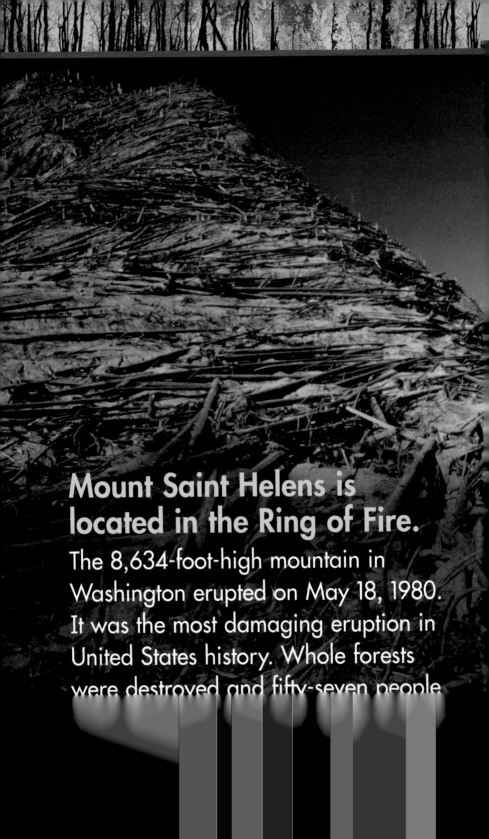

Mount Saint Helens is located in the Ring of Fire. The 8,634-foot-high mountain in Washington erupted on May 18, 1980. It was the most damaging eruption in United States history. Whole forests were destroyed and fifty-seven people

How Big?

The biggest volcano in the world is Mauna Loa in Hawaii. The mountain rises 30,000 feet above the ocean floor.

After Mount Saint Helens erupted, forests were covered with volcanic ash and dust.

CHAPTER FOUR

All Steamed

People who live near volcanoes can learn to stay safe. They can pay attention to a volcano's signals. The best protection from an eruption is to get out of harm's way. People can't stop the powerful giants from exploding. But they can learn to live with them.

People flee as Mount Pinatubo in the Philippines erupts in June 1991.

Up

Swimmers enjoy the warm waters of a volcanic crater in Deception Lake, Antarctica.

This power plant in Iceland sends heated water to the city of Reykjavik.

Scientists are looking for new ways to use volcanic power. Hot magma can be used to produce electricity. In some countries, such as Iceland, steam from volcanoes heats homes.

Volcanoes can create new land.
In 1963 an eruption under the Atlantic Ocean formed a tiny island called Surtsey. This island is named for Surtur, a giant of fire in Icelandic mythology.

A volcano erupts
on Surtsey in 1965.

The island of
Surtsey is located
near Iceland.

Hawaii's fertile fields are ideal for farming.

Ash from volcanoes enriches soil for farming.

Volcanic activity helps produce valuable minerals such as gold and silver. Rock from volcanoes can be used to build houses. Volcanoes are powerful sources of change all around the world.

Did You Know?

- The word *volcano* comes from Vulcan, the Roman god of fire.

- Scientists have discovered volcanoes on Mars and Venus.

- Jupiter's moon Io is home to at least eight active volcanoes.

- Many eruptions happen underwater. The Earth's oceans may hold as many as 10,000 volcanoes.

- About one-tenth of the people on the planet live within what scientists call the "danger range" of a volcano.

- Crushed volcanic rock is used in some toothpastes, cleaning products, and concrete.

- Fifty volcanoes have erupted in the United States.

Heat rises from a volcanic vent in the Pacific Ocean.

WORDS to Know

Active:
a volcano that is
erupting or could
erupt at any time

Lava:
hot liquid rock o
the earth's surfa

Dormant:
a volcano that has
not erupted in
hundreds of years,
but is still capable
of erupting

Magma:
hot liquid rock
underneath the
earth's surface

Extinct:
a volcano that
has not erupted in
thousands of years
and can no
longer erupt

**Tectonic
plate:**
one of the seven
major movable
pieces of the
earth's crust

FUN FACTS 4 TYPES OF VOLCANOE

1

Cinder Cone
A cone-shaped
volcano formed by
ashes and cinder

2

**Composite or
Stratovolcano**
A volcano made from
layers of ash, lava,
and volcanic debris

3

Lava Dome
A volcano with a
mound or mounds
formed by
piled-up lava

4

Shield Volca
A volcano wit
broad slope b
by hardened la
of cooled lav

32